# Dinosaur mazes

# Dinosaur mazes

maze craze

Don-Oliver
Matthies

Sterling Publishing Co., Inc.
New York

**Library of Congress-in-Publication Data Available**

10   9   8   7   6   5   4   3   2   1

Published in 2004 by Sterling Publishing Co., Inc.
387 Park Avenue South
New York, NY 10016
Originally published in Germany in 2003 under the title
*Im Land der Dinosaurier* by Edition Bücherbär im Arena
Verlag GmbH, Rottendorfer Str. 16, D-97074 Würzburg
Copyright © 2003 by Edition Bücherbär im Arena Verlag GmbH
English translation © 2004 by Sterling Publishing Co., Inc.
Distributed in Canada by Sterling Publishing
c/o Canadian Manda Group, One Atlantic Avenue, Suite 105
Toronto, Ontario, Canada M6K 3E7
Distributed in Great Britain and Europe by Chris Lloyd at Orca Book
Services, Stanley House, Fleets Lane, Poole BH15 3AJ, England
Distributed in Australia by Capricorn Link (Australia) Pty Ltd.
P.O. Box 704, Windsor, NSW 2756, Australia

Sterling ISBN 1-4027-1292-8

Draw a picture or place a
photograph of yourself
here.

This book belongs to:

_____

This is Julie, a bone-a-fide
dinosaur expert. Come join
her on a dinosaur adventure!

Here in the desert, Julie and her workers dig for dinosaur remains.

Julie digs her way down below the Earth's surface, hunting for fossilized skeletons. Can you find your way through this maze of bones?

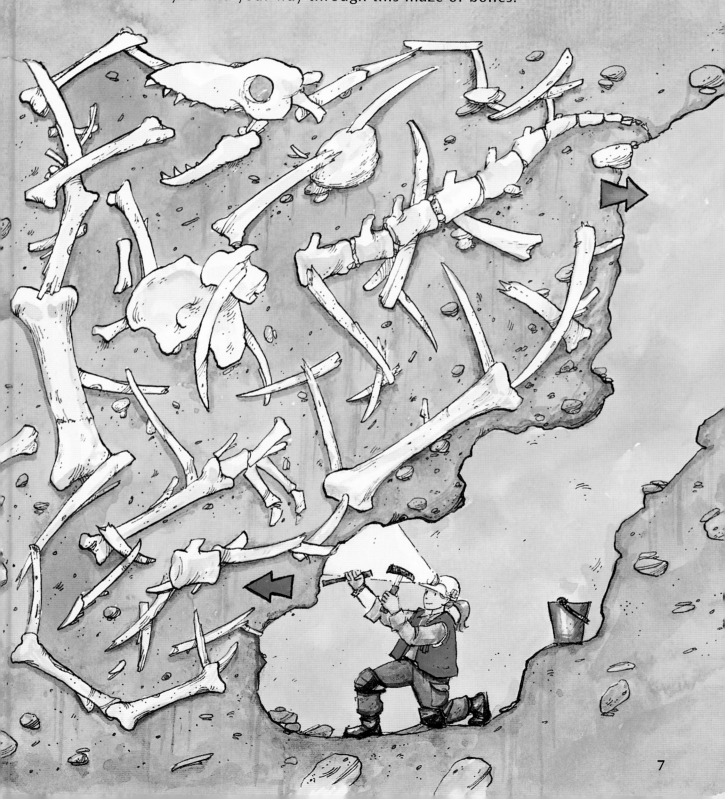

After a long day of searching, she carefully packs up the fossils and heads for the museum.

end

start

The next morning, Julie and the other scientists try to piece together a skeleton. Where do these big bones belong?

Afterwards, Julie makes a small wire model of the skeleton. She uses clay to model muscles, skin, and scales on top of the wire. She will then have a small replica of what the dinosaur probably looked like when it was alive.

Any dinosaur expert must know their dinosaur names. Can you match the correct names to these dinosaurs?

Tyrannosaurus

Stegosaurus

Pterosaurus

Brachiosaurus

Protoceratops

Julie's new dinosaur is now ready to be displayed in a special exhibit in the museum.

Today, Julie is giving a lecture on dinosaurs. "Dinosaurs dominated our world millions of years ago," she explains. "They have been extinct for many, many years."

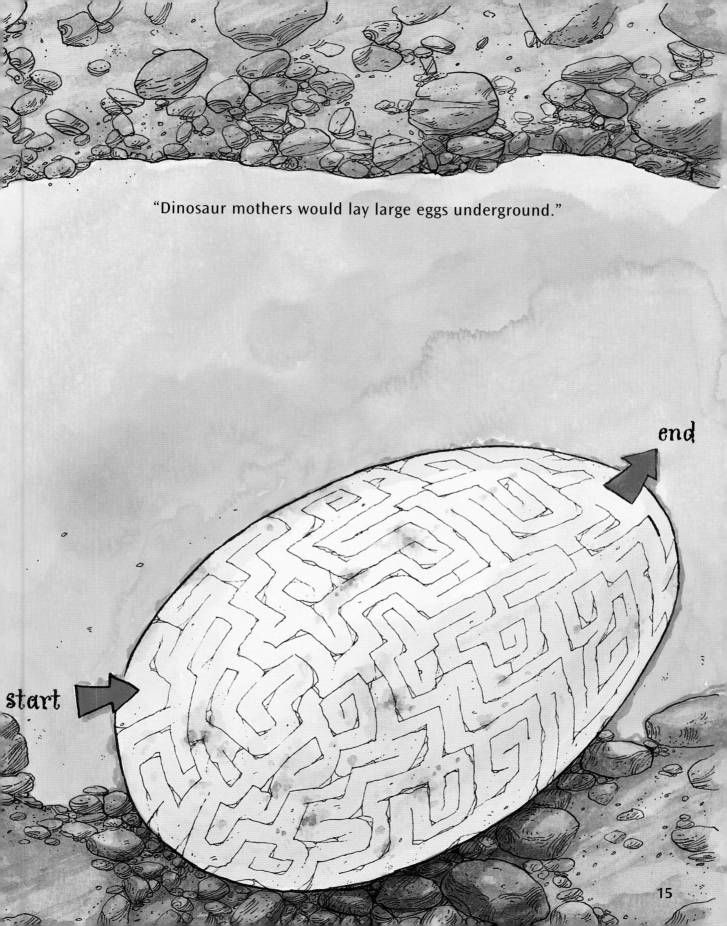

"Dinosaur mothers would lay large eggs underground."

end

start

"When the dinosaur babies would hatch from the eggs, they would have to dig their way to the surface."

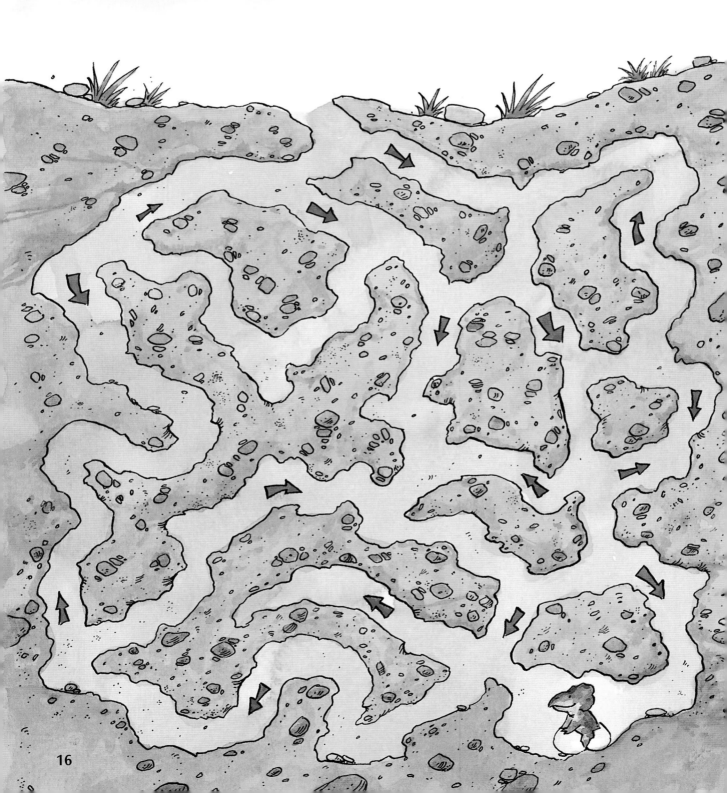

"Most dinosaurs were herbivores, which means they ate plants, trees, leaves, and ferns."

"In order to reach the tastiest leaves in the treetops, certain dinosaurs had very long necks, such as the Brachiosaurus. However, their long necks sometimes got them into trouble."

"Some dinosaurs were carnivores, which means they ate meat. The Tyrannosaurus was one of the world's greatest predators. His razor-sharp teeth were six inches long!"

"The little dinosaurs would seek protection from the predators," Julie said. Can you help the baby dinosaur find its mom?

start

end

21

"Stegosaurus had spines along its back and tail, which allowed it to defend itself against predators such as Tyrannosaurus."

start

end

start

end

"A mighty Triceratops, by the same token, would use its three great horns to defend itself against a predatory dinosaur."

"Dinosaurs did not simply dominate the land. They ruled the skies too!" Can you figure out where each Pterodactyl began its flight?

"Some dinosaurs even lived in the water, like the Plesiosaurus."

"Dinosaurs became extinct many millions of years ago." "How?" asked a student in the audience. "We do not know for certain how," explained Julie. "There are many different theories about why and how the dinosaurs became extinct. One is that there was a great volcanic eruption."

"We learn most of what we know about dinosaurs from bones that are found in the ground. A dead dinosaur would sink to the ocean floor and become covered in mud. On top of the mud, more and more layers of earth settled, and the pressure from the mud made the bones as hard as rock. Since the bones were so well preserved by this process, we can continue to find bones today."

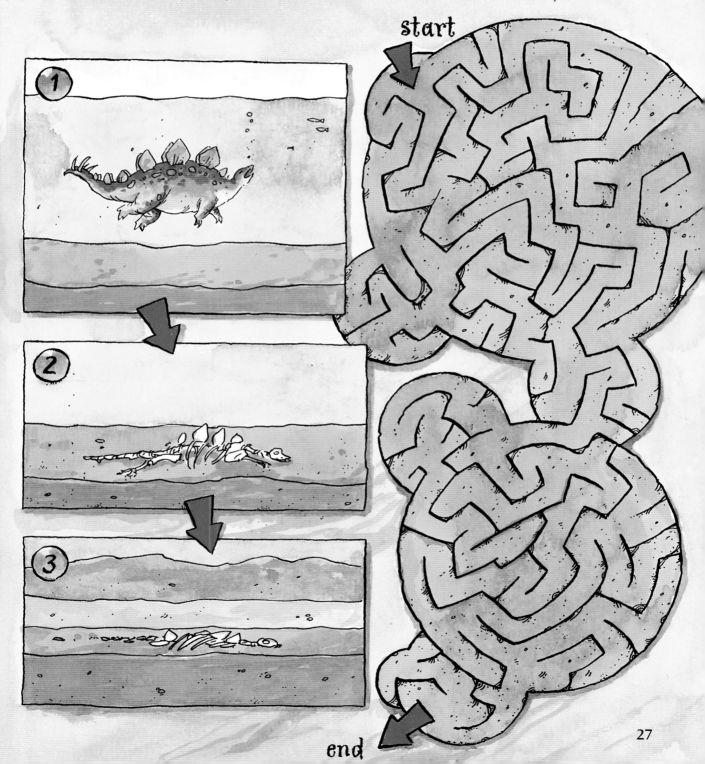

"Another theory is that a large meteorite hit the Earth. Hopefully one day we will know for sure why these great creatures became extinct!"

start

"Even though they may be extinct, dinosaurs are still with us. We can see them in movies, amusement parks, and museums."

end

start

31

"Here in the museum," said Julie, "you can learn a lot more about dinosaurs. They are some of the most wondrous creatures in history." Can you get from Start to End by walking across only the Tyrannosaurs?

Later that day, all the museum guests had a party and continued to talk about dinosaurs, thanks to Julie's exciting lecture.

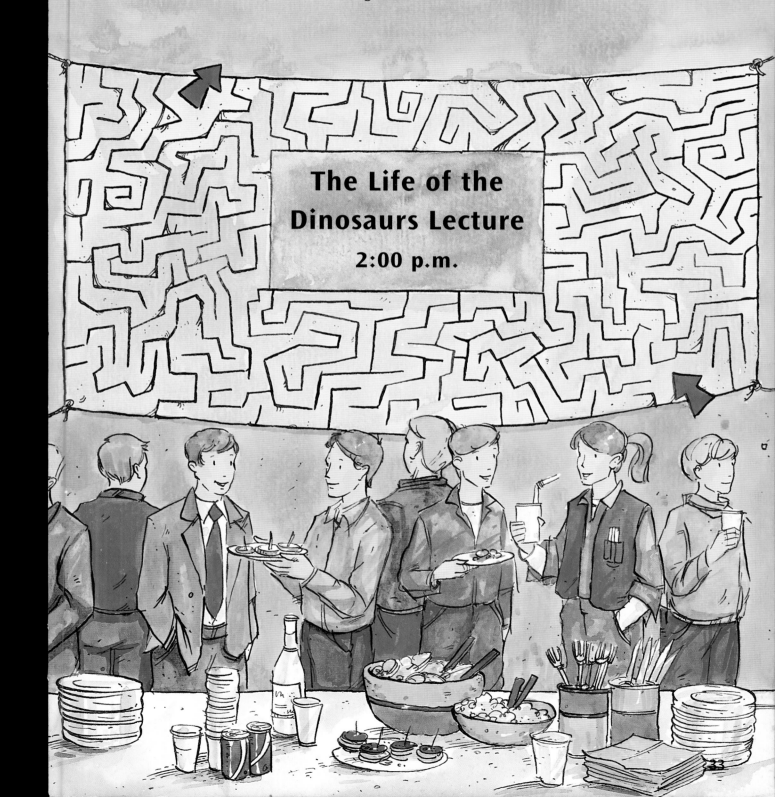

**The Life of the Dinosaurs Lecture**

**2:00 p.m.**

# Answers

page 6

page 7

page 8

start

end

34

page 9

1 = A
2 = B
3 = D
4 = C
5 = E

A = Protoceratops  D = Pterosaurus
B = Tyrannosaurus  E = Stegosaurus
C = Brachiosaurus

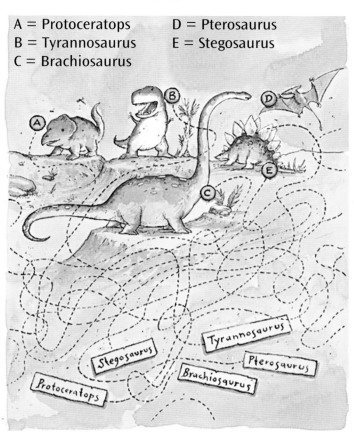

pages 12–13

35

page 14

page 15

page 16

page 17

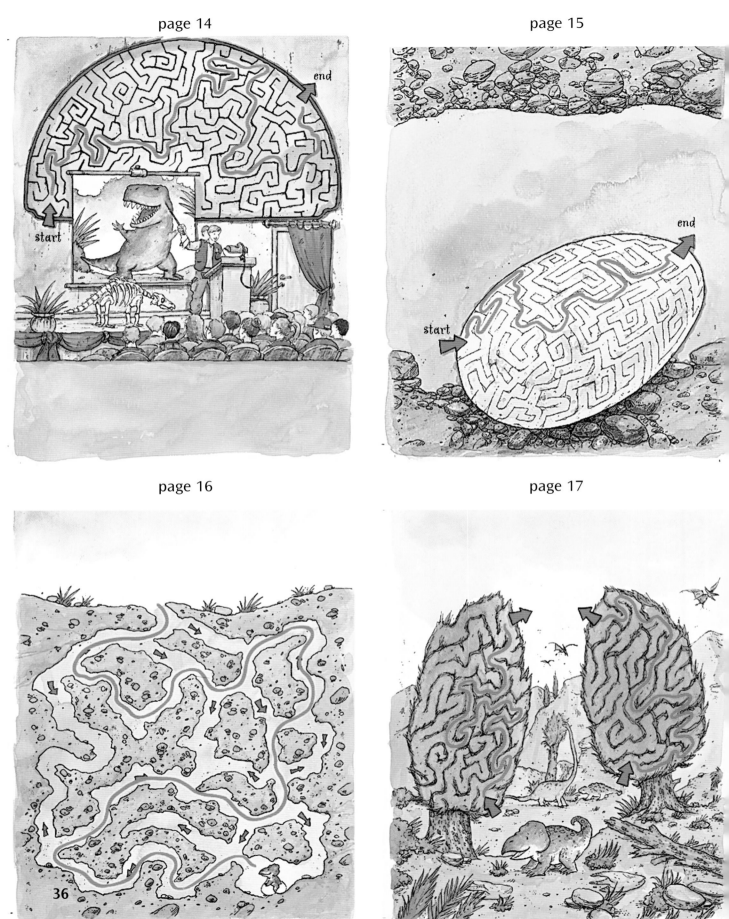

start

end

start

end

36

1 = A
2 = D
3 = C
4 = E
5 = B

pages 20–21

## page 22

## page 23

## page 24

1 = E    4 = B
2 = C    5 = D
3 = A

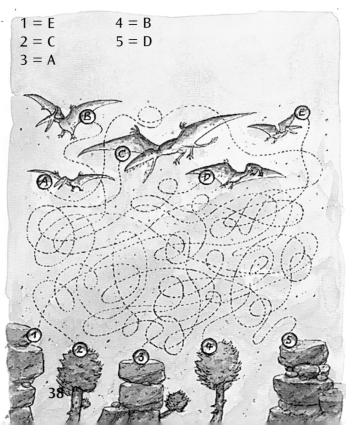

38

## page 25

page 26

end

page 27

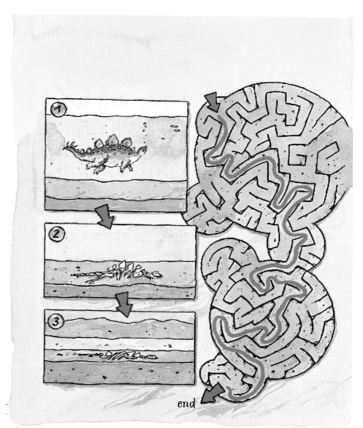

① ② ③

end

pages 28–29

start

end

39

start

end

end

start

40

**The Life of the Dinosaurs Lecture 2:00 p.m.**